MATHS FOR PARENTS

MATHS FOR PARENTS

Rosemary Russell

Piccadilly Press • London

Phototypeset from author's disk by Piccadilly Press.
Printed and bound by Martin the Printers Ltd., Berwick on Tweed
for the publishers Piccadilly Press Ltd.,
5 Castle Road, London NW1 8PR

A catalogue record for this book is available from the
British Library

ISBN: 1 85340 398 9

Rosemary Russell lives in Dorset. She is a mathematics
specialist with a wide experience of teaching both children
an adults, and has marked GCSE mathematics examination
papers. She is married with two children.

DEDICATION

This book is dedicated to my parents. They have given me a wonderful education, and have encouraged me enormously over the years. Thank you.

ACKNOWLEDGEMENTS

Many thanks to my husband, Adrian, who has been so supportive of this whole project, and of course to James and Susannah for being understanding and patient while I have used the computer.

I would like to thank Diana Cobden, a Maths Advisor for Dorset, for her advice on the National Curriculum, and for allowing me to use extracts from her excellent booklet, "Helping Children With Maths At Home".

I would also like to thank the following schools for their help in my research:

Branksome Heath County Middle School
Corfe Castle First School
Lytchett Matravers County Primary School
Queen Elizabeth's School, Wimborne

Material from the National Curriculum is Crown Copyright and is reproduced by permission of the Controller of HMSO.

Note: All of the incidents mentioned in this book are real, but to avoid embarrassment the names of those involved (apart from myself, my husband and Sir Isaac Newton) have been changed!

CONTENTS

FOREWORD

The subject of mathematics provokes curious reactions. I know: I have watched what happens when Rosemary is asked about her work.

Last night I saw a different one: a man literally unbuttoning his cuffs and making a symbolic gesture of rolling up his sleeves for a fight. Clearly we had touched something about which he felt strongly. He represents one group of people for whom we hope this book will be useful, as Rosemary explains what is going on in maths teaching today, and why.

On the whole, though, as conversation-stoppers go, "I'm a maths teacher" is pretty potent. Hardly anyone responds, "That must be fun. Tell me more ..."

The most common reaction is something like, "Oh, I was hopeless at maths ..." and a few vague expressions of awe followed by an abrupt change of subject. Sometimes they don't say anything; you just feel the temperature drop by ten degrees!

Many people seem to have fallen into a bog as far as maths is concerned; somehow they were left behind as the teacher and the rest of the class rushed on and disappeared into the gloom, and for the rest of their education they floundered uncertainly and unhappily in the morass. They learned to make a joke of it, until they saw their children heading for the same bog and found themselves unable to help.

Help is now at hand. As well as being the most fantastic wife, Rosemary is a gifted maths teacher. She cares passionately about maths, and she cares passionately about those who have got lost. She also feels strongly about the role of parents in their children's education!

We both hope that this book will bring help, encouragement and hope to all parents and maths teachers.

Adrian Russell

Christmas Eve 1995

INTRODUCTION: HELP!!!

There are many reasons why parents today find it difficult to help their children with their maths homework. This book aims to help them.

"IT ALL SEEMS DIFFERENT NOW"

Some parents were "good at maths at school", and yet when faced with modern teaching methods and ways of approaching certain simple processes, they are confused, and very frustrated. It's all different, and seems long winded. They cannot understand what their children are doing, and why things have changed! This book should help you to understand what is going on.

"I WAS NEVER ANY GOOD AT MATHS"

Then there are those parents for whom maths was always a closed book. They said goodbye to maths at some stage in their schooling, possibly early on. Now their children are stuck and they are unable to help.

To you, let me first say this:

YOU MAY NOT BE AS BAD AT MATHS AS YOU THINK YOU ARE!

There are several good reasons why people end up in this state.

1. FLAWED EXPLANATIONS

It is just possible that you were a better mathematician than your teacher, and you gave up at some point because what you were taught did not make sense. You thought it was your fault that you could not understand it; perhaps it was – but perhaps it was not!

For example, I show in Chapter Four that many of us (and I was one) were taught a "convenient lie" when we were taught subtraction. Although I have no direct evidence, it seems entirely possible that an able student could have lost confidence through being unable to accept such a flawed explanation. At the age of about eight you are more likely to think you are at fault than the teacher, and conclude that you are "no good at maths".

2. MISSING A CRUCIAL STEP

Maths is a subject that depends very heavily on you understanding each stage. It's like stacking a child's building bricks to make a wall – if you miss out a brick at any level the result can be quite dramatic if you then attempt to build up from that level. It is likely that everything above will collapse. You could have missed a stage due to illness, not getting on with your teacher, not listening during a vital lesson, or being taught in a way that did not make sense; and suddenly you were lost and you said goodbye to maths. Your reaction is quite understandable. This book may fill some gaps, and you may be surprised how much you suddenly begin to understand.

3. NO EXPLANATION GIVEN

For some, the point of departure from maths was when you were told to learn a rule or a method without any explanation at all. "I said 'cheerio' to maths at long division," is how one person described her experience, and the same thing could easily have happened to me. As I recall, I was taught it in a way in which no explanation was given, just a set of rules (technically known as an algorithm), and I was OK – but for some that was not enough. Incidentally, a quite senior educationalist recently told me that even he had never seen a written explanation for the procedure for long division. I tackle that in Chapter Seven.

MAKE A FRESH START

You may find that now, away from pressures of the classroom or looming exams, seeing these basic processes from an adult point of view will make sense, and open up maths for you again. I can assure you maths is a very enjoyable and reasonable subject (though you may not believe me yet!).

If at any time while reading the book you become

stuck, I suggest you put the book aside for a while and come back to it later. The thought processes for maths require great concentration and one can suffer from overload. You may sometimes need to back-track a bit.

Working through the examples is important. You may feel that you understand something while you are reading it, but if you move on without doing some examples you may find that your knowledge is not firmly enough established to use as a starting point for other ideas. Each brick in the wall needs to be properly placed.

BACKGROUND OF THE AUTHOR

I am an honours graduate in Pure Maths, Probability and Statistics, with a Post Graduate Certificate of Education. I have taught at a comprehensive school and a secondary modern school, lectured at a college of further education, designed and run courses for adults, given private tuition (9-year-olds up to first year university level), and marked GCSE maths examination papers.

I have also had the advantage of having a career break from teaching when my children were younger. I owned and ran my own fashion business from home for five exciting years. I staged and compèred 10 fashion shows and had a TV appearance in connection with my business. Being out of teaching for a while, in the business world, I was able to look more objectively at education and I found myself realistically questioning some of the philosophies and practices I had taken on board during my teacher training.

I can identify with the concerns of parents, and their frustration at what they see as a waste of time; yet I also appreciate what the educationalists are trying to achieve, and I hope that when you have read this book you will too.

Part 1

METHODS OF EDUCATION

Chapter 1

ROTE LEARNING VERSUS UNDERSTANDING

In maths teaching in schools there has been a very strong move away from rote learning towards learning with understanding, wherever possible.

WHAT IS LEARNING WITH UNDERSTANDING?

We recently had some friends housesit for us and look after the pets while we were away on holiday. We discovered when we returned that they had had difficulty in working out how to light our rather ancient gas oven. They had always used an electric oven, and had never used a gas oven before; and ours, ancient though it might be, does have a safety valve which prevents gas from flowing if the oven is not alight. How then can you get gas to flow to start with? It took a few days to solve the mystery. Tony, being a practical man and not to be beaten, eventually worked out what was required by using principles gleaned from years of experience of various other appliances. He was able to adapt and apply his knowledge to a totally new situation. Fortunately, to light the oven did not require a fully detailed knowledge of how the appliance worked, just a few basic principles – for example, there must be some valve that controls the flow of gas. Obviously to tackle something more advanced, he would need a much deeper knowledge of how the oven worked, but for this situation, that was not required.

Tony's response to the situation is a good example of the benefits of learning with understanding, as opposed to rote learning.

Understanding the key principles involved, he was able to use these successfully when faced with an unfamiliar situation.

WHAT IS ROTE LEARNING?

When you learn by rote, you just learn to do a task by blindly following a set of rules. You do not know why you are following these rules, or if there is any connection between them. Since you do not know why you are doing things in a certain way or order, you cannot be sure what to do when faced with something that appears slightly different. For example, suppose you had learnt to light a gas oven by using rote learning. The first instruction might have been to turn the red knob. If the colour of the oven controller is different in the model in front of you, and there is no red knob, you are stuck.

Since you do not know why you are following these

instructions, you cannot work out how to proceed. You are not prepared for an unfamiliar situation. A new set of rules is required. So rote learning has not helped you in the use of other appliances: it may even reinforce your view that appliances are frustrating things.

THE PROBLEMS OF ROTE LEARNING

There are a lot of disadvantages of learning mathematics as a set of unconnected rote-learnt rules:

i.   there would be an awful lot to learn

ii. since you cannot cover every eventuality, it is not preparing you for unfamiliar situations

iii. you do not develop a mathematical understanding, and an overall picture of maths.

THE ADVANTAGES OF LEARNING WITH UNDERSTANDING

On the other hand, if you understand the underlying principles,

i.   there is far less to remember as you understand what you are doing

ii. you are then able to transfer and apply these principles to unfamiliar situations

iii. your mathematical understanding develops and grows, enabling you to explore beyond what you have been taught.

Maths is a set of inter-related ideas, and it does make sense. It is also a toolkit which can be used to analyse and solve many different types of problems in real life. It may at first take longer and require more patience to learn with understanding, but in the long run there are many benefits.

NO TRICKERY

For many of us, maths at school seemed to be a succession of clever tricks. These days, children are encouraged to learn with understanding. The tendency is away from just learning rules without reasons for the rules. "No trickery," is how I have heard maths teaching these days described.

Parents often feel that the methods their children use seem long winded. However, when questioned, the parents might not be able to explain why their own methods work, or what they are doing. Often they have learnt rules by rote, and cannot see the connection between what they learnt and what the children are doing.

The key issue is this:

> *THERE IS OFTEN MORE THAN ONE WAY TO*
> *APPROACH A CALCULATION.*

It may seem surprising to some parents that there is often more than one correct way of tackling a maths question. Possibly in the past there has been too much emphasis on imposing the teacher's way of doing a task, and not giving room for other equally valid methods.

Some educationalists suggest that children should actually be encouraged to think around a subject, and sometimes experiment to find their own ways of working out a problem, before being given a standard procedure.

Parents have to recognise that their way is not the only way; they are not wrong, and nor is the school. In this light there need not be a confrontation, but instead a partnership and respect between school and parents.

WHEN MATHS BECAME DIFFICULT

As an adult, studying basic mathematical processes and understanding them (rather than just knowing them by rote) can open up new concepts and new lines of thought. In fact, it could help those who were good at maths until at some point, for no apparent reason, they suddenly began to find maths difficult. You can get a long way in maths by just learning rules; unfortunately, in doing so you might have missed appreciating certain concepts which were needed later.

It appears that some people do suddenly get stuck. They keep trying the only way they know in maths, which is to learn more rules. Ultimately, of course, this is not going to help. They need to start on fresh lines of thought, and looking again at basic mathematical processes can open up these new lines.

Chapter 2

THE ENQUIRING MIND

WHY WASTE TIME?

We had gone around to some friends for supper one evening and Peter, our host, was annoyed at what he considered was a complete waste of time. We were discussing the fact that his 13-year-old daughter did not yet know how to calculate the circumference of a circle. It appeared that she was doing a lot of practical work measuring circumferences of circles and calculating the result of the circumference divided by the diameter. As a maths specialist, I was able to explain to him that rather than just being told how to find the circumference of the circle, Fiona was hopefully seeing for herself that no matter what size the circle is, if you divide the circumference by the diameter, you arrive at roughly the same number – a number which we call Pi, written π. He had been taught how to find the circumference, Fiona might discover it for herself!

I have a lot of sympathy for parents. They want the best for their children's maths education, and want to help them but are puzzled and frustrated by what they see happening.

INVESTIGATIONS

Peter's reaction is typical of many parents' reactions. They are puzzled when they see their children doing in maths lessons what they consider a waste of time, what teachers call "investigations".

Investigative work can be useful and very interesting, based partly on the philosophy that if you find out for yourself, you will remember it all the more. It is also (hopefully) helping to spark an inquisitive mind and teaching techniques of investigation which pupils can use for themselves in other situations.

The other side of the coin is this: what happens if in the investigation you never find out the answer and draw the right conclusions, as you do not have the capability to do so? So much time has been possibly wasted, and frustration generated in pupil, teacher and parent.

DRAWING ANSWERS FROM PUPILS

Another parent, Jenny, a governor at a local first school regularly went in to help in a class. During maths activities, the teacher had given her specific instructions not to tell the children the answers to their questions, but draw the answer from them. Jenny confessed to her frustration; she longed to be able to just tell them.

This type of teaching technique is used in other subjects too. What's going on in this situation? The idea is that by drawing answers from pupils by asking suitable questions, you are leading them rather than telling them, or as some might say, "not handing it to them on a platter". In this way you are making the children think and make use of their store of knowledge.

WHAT ABOUT OUR CULTURAL HERITAGE?

It can be asked, what is wrong with just telling them? After all, it is only by your skill in asking suitable questions that they have been led. Could they be deceived into thinking they have come to the conclusion by themselves, and therefore have all the answers within? Is this conducive to them learning to ask their elders and betters for advice? By being taught (or having it handed to them on a platter) pupils are acknowledging and making use of the accumulated wisdom of (possibly) centuries. It is part of our cultural heritage.

Sir Isaac Newton said, "If I have seen a little farther than others, it is because I have stood on the shoulders of giants." The works of earlier mathematicians and scientists were available to him. When the philosophy is for children to be encouraged to develop their own methods of carrying out a calculation, and they are not taught in recognisable ways (it is worth noting the National Curriculum does not require children to know or use any specific algorithm), parents may well ask, "Is our cultural heritage being wasted? Why waste time in rediscovering the wheel or finding a new way to subtract?" Why indeed!

POSSIBLE ANSWERS

Some possible answers were given in a discussion pamphlet published by Her Majesty's Inspectors of Schools in 1979.

"The belief that children should be enabled to discover important mathematical ideas for themselves has been developed over many years in numerous publications... Discovery methods are a sound approach when they are used to lead children to acquire a deeper understanding of the processes involved and more enthusiasm for the subject. *Of course, neither teachers nor children have the time or skill to ensure that children discover everything* but, if their future attitudes to the subject are to be positive, it is important that each should have sufficient experience of personal discovery."[1]

"Today, the child is encouraged to make enquiries, investigate, discover and record; *learning is not looked upon only as something imposed from without.* It is recognised that it is through his own activity that the child is able to form the new concepts which will in turn be the basis of further mathematical ideas and thinking."[2]

We learn in a mixture of ways. One way may be through making the discovery for ourselves; another way is by directly learning from specific instruction from someone else who has a particular skill (e.g. how to bake a particular cake).

There would be greater respect, support, co-operation and understanding between parents and maths teachers if:

i.   Parents could appreciate the importance of personal discovery and practical work.

ii. Educationalists remembered not to waste time, first-ly by not trying to let the children discover everything since, "... neither teacher nor children have the time or skill to ensure that children discover everything ..."[1] And secondly, as "... learning is not looked upon *only* as something imposed from without ..."[2] implies, realistically, that at times it does have to be imposed from without. This means, in practical terms, that at times it is OK to answer questions directly!

Chapter 3

THE NATIONAL CURRICULUM

STRUCTURE OF THE NATIONAL CURRICULUM

The National Curriculum applies to all students of compulsory school age in maintained schools in England and Wales. This includes grant-maintained schools and grant-maintained special schools. It dictates which subjects are to be taught. Mathematics is one of the few subjects that all children have to study.

TERMS USED

The National Curriculum is organised broadly into what are known as *Key Stages,* and there are four of these. The pupils' age dictates which Key Stage they belong to. A rough guide to the ages is as follows:

Key Stage 1	5-7 years old	Year Groups 1-2
Key Stage 2	7-11 years old	Year Groups 3-6

Key Stage 3   11-14 years old   Year Groups 7-9

Key Stage 4   14-16 years old   Year Groups 10-11

For maths, at each key stage there is what is known as a *programme of study*. This sets out what pupils should be given opportunities to do, and also what they should be taught. *Attainment targets* set out the expected standards of the pupil's performance.

The programmes of study are split into different areas. Let us look more closely at the programmes of study for the different key stages.

KEY STAGE 1

The programme of study is split into *three* basic areas. We need to remember that the areas are interrelated, and are not totally separate. These areas are:

USING AND APPLYING MATHEMATICS

This is basically about the processes. In other words, how you go about things. For example, choosing the correct equipment or material to do a task, the mathematics to use and how to record their work, becoming familiar with mathematical language and symbols, e.g. "+".

This section says at the very beginning that pupils should be given opportunities to:

"Use and apply mathematics in practical tasks, in real-life

problems and within mathematics itself." (National Curriculum p.2)

NUMBER (INCLUDES ALGEBRA AND DATA HANDLING)

Pupils learn about our number system. They should be taught to, *"Develop a variety of methods for adding and subtracting."* (National Curriculum p.3). Algebra is studied in terms of looking for number patterns, or patterns of shapes. They solve problems using numbers. They study data handling, for example by sorting and classifying objects by size, shape and mass.

SHAPE, SPACE AND MEASURES

They should be taught about common 2-D and 3-D shapes, how to recognise right angles, and standard units of length, to name but a few topics. The subject of measures is one in which parents can play a particularly useful part, and I shall discuss this in Chapter Nine.

This has been only a very brief look at the programme of study for Key Stage 1, and is by no means a full summary.

KEY STAGE 2

The programme of study is split into *four* basic areas for this stage. Once again, we need to remember that the areas are interrelated, and are not totally separate. These areas are:

USING AND APPLYING MATHEMATICS

The areas covered in Key Stage 1 are built upon and expanded. For example, *"Pupils should be taught to ... explain their reasoning."* (National Curriculum p.6)

NUMBER (AND ALGEBRA)

The areas covered in Key Stage 1 are built upon and extended. For example, use of decimals, multiplication facts (tables) to 10x10, percentages; pupils use formulae which have been expressed in words (see Chapter 12), leading on eventually to using letters as symbols; " ... *understand multiplication as repeated addition, and division as sharing and repeated subtraction; use associated language and recognise situations to which the operations apply ... "* (National Curriculum p.8); they should be taught how to use a basic calculator, and check whether the answer thus obtained is reasonable.

SHAPE, SPACE AND MEASURES

The work covered in Key Stage 1 is built upon and extended. Symmetry, angles and how to specify a location, for example by using maps, are some of the areas studied.

HANDLING DATA

This is now a section on its own. Pupils start to understand probability in relation to every day life, e.g. is it likely to rain? They extract and interpret information from simple tables. They carry out surveys. *"Pupils should be given opportunities to use computers as a source of interesting data, and as a tool for representing data."* (National Curriculum p.10).

Once again, this is by no means a complete summary of the programme of study for Key Stage 2, just a brief look.

KEY STAGES 3 AND 4

For these stages, the programme of study is split into *five* areas. Again, remember that the areas are not totally separate, and do interrelate. They are:

USING AND APPLYING MATHEMATICS

The work covered in Key Stages 1 and 2 is built upon and extended.

NUMBER

The work covered in Key Stages 1 and 2 is built upon and extended.

ALGEBRA
This is now a separate section, but builds upon what has gone before in Key Stages 1 and 2. One of the areas covered is that pupils should be taught to solve a range of equations, including the use of trial-and-improvement methods.

SHAPE, SPACE AND MEASURES
Pupils build on and extend the work done in Key Stages 1 and 2. Areas covered by this section include finding the circumference and area of circles, trigonometry, Pythagoras' theorem.

HANDLING DATA
The work done in Key Stages 1 and 2 is built upon and extended.

This has been a quick glance at the programme of study for Key Stages 3 and 4, and is not intended as a complete summary.

QUESTIONS AND ANSWERS ABOUT THE NATIONAL CURRICULUM

The following questions may arise, and so I shall deal with them.

CAN YOU TELL ME ABOUT NATIONAL CURRICULUM TESTING?

At the end of each Key Stage, teachers make an assessment of the *level* (see below) at which they think each pupil is performing.

Teachers assess continually as pupils progress through the programmes of study, but at the end of each Key Stage, there is a formal assessment by the teacher to establish the level the pupils have attained. There are also *Statutory End of Key Stage Tasks and Tests* which are externally set. At Key Stage 1 these are marked by teachers but at Key Stages 2 and 3 they are externally marked. Levels are also given for these Tasks and Tests.

The teacher's assessment and the Tasks and Tests result are then sent off, and together using a computer programme, an overall level is given to each pupil.

Where there is a discrepancy between the two, from the academic year 1995-6, the teacher's assessment has priority over the Tasks and Tests result.

WHAT IS A "LEVEL?"

A "level" roughly describes what sort of things a child is capable of doing. Each of the main areas in maths, *Using and Applying Mathematics*, *Number and Algebra*, *Shape Space and Measures*, and *Handling Data,* are split up into levels. Descriptions of the different levels are listed in the National Curriculum. For example, a pupil performing at *level 3* in *Number and Algebra* would demonstrate the following characteristics:

"Pupils show understanding of place value in numbers

up to 1000 and use this to make approximations. They have begun to use decimal notation and to recognise negative numbers, in contexts such as money, temperature and calculator displays. Pupils use mental recall of addition and subtraction facts to 20 in solving problems involving larger numbers. They use mental recall of the 2, 5 and 10 multiplication tables, and others up to 5x5, in solving whole-number problems involving multiplication or division, including those that give rise to remainders. Pupils use calculator methods where numbers include several digits. They have begun to develop mental strategies, and use them to find methods for adding and subtracting numbers with at least two digits." (National Curriculum p.25)

Remember that the descriptions start at level 1 and work upwards. So to be at level 3, they would have progressed through levels 1 and 2. (I mention this as I have heard of one case where the parent was concerned as they thought their child, who was very capable and was given level 3, should at least have been at level 1, not 3. They mistakenly believed that level 1 was higher!)

HOW DO TEACHERS DECIDE ON A LEVEL DESCRIPTION FOR MY CHILD?

This is done by looking at the pupil's work and trying to determine which level descriptions are fulfilled by the pupil.

Teachers have guidance to help judge the levels, so that there is consistency. Very often teachers will collaborate on assessment, as a form of moderation, and try to reach a consensus.

A pupil may be able to do some things which appear at a higher level, but the level given is the one that best describes the majority of their work.

"*...level descriptions describe the types and range of performance that pupils working at a particular level should characteristically demonstrate. In deciding on a pupil's level of attainment at the end of each key stage, teachers should judge which description best fits the pupil's performance. Each description should be considered in conjunction with the descriptions for adjacent levels.*" (National Curriculum p.22)

WHAT ARE THE LEVELS AT THE DIFFERENT KEY STAGES?

In a nutshell, this is a rough guide:

Key Stage 1
levels 1 to 3

Key Stage 2
levels 2 to 5 (there is an exceptional performance possibility of level 6 which would take the pupil to a secondary school programme of study)

Key Stage 3
levels 3 to 8 (there is a possibility of exceptional performance above level 8).

WHAT DOES THIS MEAN FOR MY CHILD IN, FOR EXAMPLE, NUMBER?

Remember that the level descriptions are a rough guide. The following describes the sort of work a pupil at level 2 can do:

"Pupils count sets of objects reliably, and use mental recall of addition and subtraction facts to 10. They have begun to understand the place value of each digit in a number and use this to order numbers up to 100. They choose the appropriate operation when solving addition and subtraction problems. They identify and use halves and quarters, such as half a rectangle or a quarter of eight objects. They recognise sequences of numbers, including odd and even numbers." (National Curriculum p.25)

The following describes the sort of work a pupil at level 4 can do; remember that the pupil is assumed to have achieved levels 1, 2, and 3 already:

"Pupils use their understanding of place value to multiply and divide whole numbers by 10 or 100. In solving number problems, pupils use a range of mental and written methods of computation with the four operations, including mental recall of multiplication facts up to 10 x 10. They add and subtract decimals to two places. In solving problems with or without a calculator, pupils check the reasonableness of their results by reference to their knowledge of the context or to the size of the numbers. They recognise approximate proportions of a whole and use simple fractions and percentages to describe these. Pupils explore and describe number patterns, and relationships including multiple, factor and square. They have begun to use simple formulae expressed in words. Pupils use and interpret co-ordinates in the first quadrant." (National Curriculum p.25)

WHO DECIDES WHAT SORT
OF WORK MY CHILD DOES?

The National Curriculum for maths provides a framework of what should be taught. It is up to the individual schools to interpret how this is to be put into practice. Each school has its own scheme of work. This will show what is to be covered, and the resources available at the school; for example, there may be exercises available to do in connection with a topic.

Teachers will often include maths activities in their planning for cross-curricular topics.

ARE ALL MATHS LESSONS PRESENTED
IN THE SAME WAY?

Exactly how each teacher presents the work is up to the individual. This must be allowable, otherwise teachers would be like robots, having to say the same thing!

An example may be called for here. I recently undertook some observation at a comprehensive school. The pupils were streamed for ability, and in one year group, I moved from set to set. In two of the sets, the students were investigating plotting and drawing straight line graphs and simple curves. The groups concerned were both doing this investigation, but how that was put into practice was up to the individual teacher.

One group was plotting the graphs on their own, with the teacher moving around the class, discussing the work with individuals. There were some interesting(!) looking graphs. In the other group, the teacher and pupils were plotting the graphs together, with the teacher using the blackboard to plot his graph. Both groups were carrying out an investigation, but in different ways.

The teacher, who is on the spot, can assess the best approach for each group, and even use different styles of teaching in a lesson. Of course, the equipment available at a school can also affect the way a topic is presented.

WHAT SORT OF THINGS MIGHT I FIND STRANGE IN MY CHILD'S MATHS LESSONS?

In the earlier years there tends to be a lot of practical work, which may come as a surprise. Sometimes it may seem that they are only playing games, but the tasks they are doing in the games are making them use their mathematical knowledge and reasoning power.

Many text books that I have seen recently are very much more attractive and colourful than those used in the past, and they use everyday situations rather than abstract questions.

To some it may also seem strange that children are enjoying their maths lessons!

WHAT HAPPENS IF WE CHANGE SCHOOLS?

Be aware that there may be a slightly different approach at the new school. There may be more, or less, practical work. It takes time to adjust to new teachers, a new setting, and so on. It may be a good idea to take a sample of the sort of work your child has been doing for the new maths teacher to see.

HOW ARE THE TASKS' AND TESTS' LEVELS DECIDED?

The National Curriculum covers *all* maintained schools, including special schools. The Tasks and Tests, which are externally set, therefore have to cater for all ranges of ability.

Let us look at each Key Stage separately.

Key Stage 1

Pupils at level 1 are assessed by practical tasks. Other pupils do tests. Results of these are usually in levels 1-3. There is the possibility of a higher level, after further testing, for those of exceptional performance.

Key Stage 2

Pupils at Levels 1-2 are assessed by practical tasks. Other pupils sit tests, (on a set date in the summer term), with 2 papers, with outcomes in Levels 3-5. For those of exceptional performance, there is a possibility of taking an extension paper, and being given a higher level than 5. If pupils fail to achieve level 3 on tests, they are awarded level 2.

Key Stage 3

Pupils at Levels 1-2 are assessed by practical tasks. Other pupils sit exams with 2 papers. The exams are set at 4 tiers; each tier is geared to give outcomes within a certain range of levels. The tiers are:

Levels   3-5 (outcome of level 2 is also possible)
Levels   4-6
Levels   5-7
Levels   6-8 (For those of exceptional performance,

there is the possibility of sitting an extension paper, and being given a higher level than 8)

WHAT HAPPENS AT KEY STAGE 4?

The main way of testing is for pupils to sit a GCSE examination.

Whereas up to Key Stage 3 the Tasks and Tests are set nationally, there are many different boards that set GCSE exams, and it is up to individual schools to decide which board they choose to use. The pupil's GCSE may include some coursework as well as exams, depending on the syllabus chosen. Pupils are given a grade as a result of the whole examination.

There are three tiers of entry at GCSE. Here is a guide to the outcomes available for each tier.

Foundation/Basic Tier: Grades G, F, E and D (exceptionally C may be awarded)

Intermediate/Central Tier: Grades F, E, D, C and B (exceptionally A may be awarded)

Higher/Further Tier: Grades D, C, B, A and A*

WHO DECIDES WHICH KEY STAGE 3 TIER AND GCSE TIER MY CHILD TAKES?

This decision is made by the teacher's assessment of which exam will best cater for your child's ability.

The exams are set for different levels, and designed to give outcomes that are within a certain range.

IF MY CHILD WANTS TO GO ON TO FURTHER EDUCATION, WHICH GRADE WILL THEY NEED?

They would usually need at least a grade C. I would check with their maths teacher the grades available in the tier your child is to sit.

HOW CAN I WORK TOGETHER WITH THE SCHOOL, AND HELP MY CHILD WITH THEIR TASKS AND TESTS?

You need to know that the Tasks and Tests are not reams and reams of straightforward calculations, but are designed to test the pupil's ability to use mathematics and also to use mathematical language.

The questions are often set in such a way that each child has to extract for themselves, from the information given, what to do. For example, they may need to explain what they are doing. Encouraging them to explain how they arrive at an answer is one way you can help.

Make maths part of everyday life. I discuss this in Chapter Nine.

Try not to be anxious, and have a positive attitude towards maths!

Remember, if you have any queries or worries, do ask the child's teacher.

Part 2

SOME KEY AREAS OF CONFUSION

Chapter 4

TAKE AWAY THE CONFUSION:
A CLOSE LOOK AT SUBTRACTION

TWO METHODS: NOT MANY PEOPLE
KNOW THIS ...

"You know, I never really understood what was going on," confessed Tim, as I was giving him some maths lessons. He had changed schools a few years earlier and had encountered something of which not many people are aware:

$$\begin{array}{r} 4\,7 \\ -2\,9 \\ \hline \\ \hline \end{array}$$

THERE ARE TWO MAIN METHODS OF SUBTRACTION USING "PENCIL AND PAPER"

Both methods are valid, but they are very different in their approach. It came as no surprise to me that the two schools had taught different methods of subtraction, and that Tim never really understood what was going on when he saw the second method. Unsure of the first method and confused by the second, he floundered. It is typical of the sort of trouble that people get into with maths that, in his latter years at the new school, his maths teacher was also the head-master and I don't think Tim had the courage to own up to not understanding. As I explained it to him, he understood and I believe it helped him with the rest of his mathematics as well.

When a new pupil is referred to me for lessons, one of the first things I usually check is which method of subtraction they have been taught and whether or not they have difficulty in understanding it. It is a very basic mathematical operation, but one which, surprisingly, causes many problems.

A PUZZLE FOR PARENTS

I wonder how many others in Tim's situation never had this explained to them. The two different methods have been taught for years; my husband and I were taught differently, as were my mother and father.

Subtraction is a classic example of an area where there can be conflict between parents and schools. Many parents are puzzled by their children's mathe-matics, and in particular, subtraction. They would like to help their children but are unaware of the fact that there are these two methods. If they see a method they do not recognise, they are confused; in one case I know, the child was told that the school was teaching them wrongly. Some parents try to help by teaching the method they learnt themselves, and end up only con-fusing the child (as I know from experience). Often, after I have shown parents how to subtract using the two methods, they suddenly understand the seemingly strange things that their children are trying to do.

> WORK IN PARTNERSHIP WITH THE CHILD'S
> SCHOOL SO AS NOT TO CAUSE CONFUSION!

Identify which method you have been taught, and also which method your child is being taught. When offering help, follow the method taught at the child's school so as NOT to cause confusion.

Years before, it had come as a surprise even to me to discover that there were these two methods of subtraction. I only found out while studying for my Post Graduate Certificate of Education! The two methods are known as (a) Subtraction by equal addition and (b) Subtraction by decomposition.

IDENTIFY THE METHOD

Shown below is the same subtraction, worked out using the two methods. They not only look very different but are also very different in their approach.

$$
\begin{array}{r}
4\,^17 \\
-\ 2\ 9 \\
\scriptstyle 1 \\
\hline
1\ 8
\end{array}
\qquad
\begin{array}{r}
^3\!4\,^17 \\
-\ 2\ 9 \\
\hline
1\ 8
\end{array}
$$

a. Subtraction by Equal Addition   b. Subtraction by Decomposition

SUBTRACTION BY EQUAL ADDITION

This is the method I learnt, and which will be familiar to many parents. However, it does have drawbacks in the way in which it has often been taught, using misleading jargon. Only in my teacher training did I learn that I had been taught a "convenient lie". It became clear as one of the maths lecturers urged us to do a subtraction, and to use little bricks to act out what we were saying, as part of a practical session.

"BORROW AND PAY BACK": THE CONVENIENT LIE

The lie became clear as I performed the subtraction 47-29, and started to do the working using the jargon "borrow and pay back".

i. "Seven take away nine – I can't do, so

ii. I borrow a 1 from the 2,

iii. and then pay it back.

iv. 9 from 17 is 8 ...."

$$
\begin{array}{r}
4^{1}7 \\
-\ 2\ 9 \\
_{1}\ \\
\hline
1\ 8
\end{array}
$$

But hang on! If I BORROW 1 from the 2, and I PAY IT BACK, surely there should only be 2. I obviously have not borrowed 1 from the 2, because if that is the case, when I "pay back", I should be back where I started, with 2; yet I knew that I should be taking (2+1=3) from 4 in the tens column, to obtain the correct answer of eighteen. What is going on?

The other question is, how am I able to "pay back"? What am I using to "pay back"?

"BORROW AND PAY BACK": THE TRUTH

The truth is that you do NOT borrow 1 from the 2. What you are actually doing is this:

i. ADDING one ten to the top number, giving seventeen in the units column, and

ii. ADDING one ten to the bottom number, giving three in the tens column.

$$\begin{array}{r} 4\,\overset{+10}{7} \\ -\{\underset{+1}{2}\,9 \\ \hline 1\,8 \end{array}$$

Some background information is required before we proceed with an explanation.

> *ADDING THE SAME NUMBER TO BOTH NUMBERS LEAVES THE DIFFERENCE UNALTERED*

When we calculate a subtraction, we are working out the difference between two numbers. The difference between 5 and 3 is 2. If we add one to both numbers, we would have 6 and 4: the difference between them is still 2. As long as we add the same amount to both numbers, the difference remains the same; the smaller number never catches up with the larger.

We often use this technique when calculating a subtraction mentally, finding a suitable number to add so that we make a simple calculation. For example, the difference between 83 and 27 is the same as the difference between 86 and 30, where 3 has been added to both numbers. The calculation can now be done quite simply, and gives the answer 56.

BACK TO THE CALCULATION ...

The difference between 47 and 29 is the same as that between 57 and 39. Ten has been added to each of the numbers, but in different columns. Now that you have equally added to both numbers in this way, the subtraction is possible:

i. In the units column, $17 - 9 = 8$

ii. in the tens column, $4 - 3 = 1$

In this method, you neatly add 10's in such a way as to make a subtraction possible.

Up until that practical session at Teacher Training College, I – a graduate mathematician – had been automatically subtracting and not realising what I was really doing! How many of us were taught this by rote, and did not question what was happening?

"BORROW AND PAY BACK" USED CORRECTLY

I have called the "borrow and pay back" jargon a "convenient lie" because of the way in which it is often (though not always) taught with the suggestion that we are borrowing from the 2 (using our example). I have shown that we are not.

However, I can think of one situation where the use of the jargon "borrow and pay back" is justifiable, if used correctly; and it may help to illustrate what is happening.

Let's assume I have 47 pence in my purse, in the form of 4 ten pence pieces and 7 one penny pieces. I owe you 29 pence; how much money remains in my purse after paying you back? That would need me to calculate the subtraction 47-29.

$$4\ 7^{+10}$$
$$-\left\{2\ 9\right._{+1}$$

I unfortunately do not have the correct change, but I notice you happen to have a stack of one penny coins, so I say to you, "Can I BORROW 10 pennies from you, and in the change I'll give you an extra 10 pence coin, I'll PAY YOU BACK."

Note, I have borrowed *from you*, not from the 29 pence I owe you, and adjusted the calculation accordingly!

$$4^{1}7$$
$$-\ \underset{1}{2\ 9}$$
$$1\ 8$$

CAN I CARRY ON SAYING IT WRONG?

I have been asked by a person who was taught the "convenient lie" in the equal addition method, "Is it O.K. to continue subtracting the way I have been taught?" presumably meaning, "Can I carry on saying to myself 'borrow and pay back?'" To any who are asking the same question my answer is, "Of course it is ... though perhaps now you will really understand what you are actually doing!"

SUBTRACTION BY DECOMPOSITION

The other method, decomposition, is as follows:
Seven take away nine is not possible, so

i. I change one of the tens in the tens column of the top number into ten units: I "decompose" it, just like changing a ten pence piece into ten pennies.

$$\begin{array}{r} {}^{-1}\ {}^{+10} \\ 4\ 7 \\ -\ 2\ 9 \\ \hline 1\ 8 \end{array}$$

ii. This leaves three tens in the tens column, and we add the ten units to the units column.

iii. Ten units plus seven makes seventeen in the units column, and nine from seventeen is eight.

iv. In the tens column, three tens take away two tens leaves one ten.

$$\begin{array}{r} {}^{3}\cancel{4}\ {}^{1}7 \\ -\ 2\ 9 \\ \hline 1\ 8 \end{array}$$

Please remember that both methods are valid, but they are quite different, so do not mix them up! Try using both methods yourself.

SUBTRACTION BY ADDITION (COMPLEMENTARY ADDITION)

Here is a third method that is used for working out a

subtraction. In this method we calculate the difference by counting up, in suitable stages, from one number until we reach the other number.

Let us look at the example 47-29, and use this method to calculate the answer.

i. Using the number line:

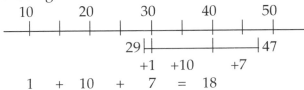

ii. Using numbers only:
   29 to 30 is 1
   30 to 40 is 10
   40 to 47 is 7
   1 + 10 + 7 is 18

iii. Later, this becomes:
   29 to 30 is 1
   30 to 47 is 17
   1 + 17 is 18

It may be of interest to know that accountants traditionally use this method when calculating a subtraction. The reasons go back 500 years.

This method is often used in giving change when shopping. In fact, playing a shopping game with your child is a very useful way of helping them with their subtraction and grasping the structure of our number system, among other mathematical areas, without them even realising it. I shall discuss this in more depth in Chapter Nine.

WHICH METHOD IS USED IN SCHOOLS?

The National Curriculum does not specify which method should be taught, but I would say that decomposition is the most likely pencil and paper method to be taught in schools these days.

It needs to be said that it is not a new method. It did not come in, as I heard someone say, with the National Curriculum. My mother and I were taught to do subtractions using equal addition, but my father and my husband were taught to use decomposition. It was only relatively recently that my father realised we subtracted differently!

You might like to ask among your family and friends and find out how others subtract. You may be surprised by the answers you get!

HARDER SUBTRACTIONS

In Chapter Six we will look at more advanced subtractions, like the one shown here, but first we need to look more closely at our number system.

$$
\begin{array}{r}
2\,0\,0\,1 \\
-\quad 9\,9 \\
\hline
 \\
\hline
\end{array}
$$

Chapter 5

WHAT'S IN A NUMBER?

WE COUNT IN TENS

I had asked Helen to write down for me two thousand and twenty. The answer she gave, as I recall, was 20020; why is it wrong? She had attempted to write the number as it is said, but her answer was incorrect. It should have been 2020. This is an area of confusion for a number of people.

What is in a number? Our number system has a clever structure which makes it very elegant and powerful. We count in batches of ten. Historically, we can see there are other ways of recording a number; for example, Roman numerals (which, by comparison, are very clumsy). In our system, each digit, by its place in the number, shows what it is worth. Zero is used to represent the absence of a certain quantity. Zero was probably introduced to the West from Hindu India in the Middle Ages and was vital in the development of a practical number system.

AN EXTRACT FROM OUR NUMBER SYSTEM

Shown below is an extract from the structure of our number system.

Tens of Thousands	Thousands	Hundreds	Tens	Units
$10^4=10000$	$10^3=1000$	$10^2=100$	$10^1=10$	$10^0=1$

A note of explanation may be needed here.

10×10 is written 10^2

$10 \times 10 \times 10$ is written 10^3

$10 \times 10 \times 10 \times 10$ is written 10^4, – and so on.

The last of these is read as, "Ten to the power of four". 10^5 is read as, "Ten to the power of five", and so on. However 10^2 is usually read, "Ten squared", and 10^3 is usually read, "Ten cubed".

10^0 is 1. Any number to the power zero is 1. The explanation for this is outside the scope of this book.

Later in this chapter, we will need to know that:

10^{-1} means $^1/_{10} = 0.1$

10^{-3} means $^1/_{1000} = 0.001$ and so on.

PLACE VALUE: THE IMPORTANCE OF POSITION

Here are some examples.

Tens of Thousands	Thousands	Hundreds	Tens	Units
$10^4=10000$	$10^3=1000$	$10^2=100$	$10^1=10$	$10^0=1$
		8	0	6
	2	0	2	0

Eight hundred and six is written as an 8 under the hundreds column; there are no tens (i.e. no twenty, or thirty etc.), therefore zero is placed under the tens column; and there are six units so six is placed under the units column.

8 x 100 = 800
0 x 10 = 0
6 x 1 = 6

Adding these together gives,
800
+ 6
___
806

In the number two thousand and twenty, there are two thousands, so 2 is placed in the thousands column; no hundreds are mentioned, so zero is placed in the hundreds column; twenty (which is two tens), is represented by 2 under the tens column; and no units are required, so a zero is placed in the units column. In any whole number, the value of the units column must be shown (even if it is zero), as by its position we can work out the value of the other digits. For example in the number 154, the 5 is worth five tens (i.e. fifty); in the number 1540, the 5 is worth five hundreds. Because we know where the units column is, we can work out the value of the other digits. For example,

2 x 1000 = 2000
0 x 100 = 0
2 x 10 = 20
0 x 1 = 0

Adding these together gives,

2000
+ 20
‾‾‾‾
2020

LARGE NUMBERS

For large numbers, a comma or a small space may be placed between each group of three numbers counting to the left from the units column. For example, 2020 can be written 2,020. This makes large numbers easier to read, but is not really part of the number system.

A LARGER EXTRACT FROM OUR NUMBER SYSTEM

Here is a larger extract from our number system, which shows more fully the pattern in the powers of ten in the structure. For a whole number we do not need to show the decimal point and following zeros, but as always, we need to show the value of the units column.

For a number that is wholly a decimal, it is customary to show the value of the units column, which would be zero. This is then followed by the decimal point and the required numbers.

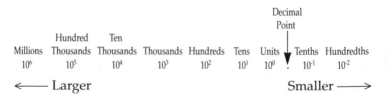

	Hundred Thousands	Ten Thousands	Thousands	Hundreds	Tens	Units	Decimal Point	Tenths	Hundredths
Millions									
10^6	10^5	10^4	10^3	10^2	10^1	10^0	.	10^{-1}	10^{-2}

⟵ Larger   Smaller ⟶

EXERCISES

Try writing these numbers in figures (answers on page 68):

(a) Four hundred and twenty-nine thousand and eight.

(b) Five million, eighty-eight thousand and fifty-six.

(c) One thousand seven hundred and sixty six.

REWRITING A NUMBER IN SMALLER UNITS

Imagine a milometer in a car. It starts at all zeros. As the miles go by, the numbers change from 0 through to 9 in the units column. To show ten miles, a one is shown in the tens column and a zero in the units column.

Eventually 99 is reached. At the end of the next mile there are:

9+1= ten units, in the units column.

This is shown as a zero in the units column, and one ten is added to the tens column.

In the tens column, there are now:

9+1 tens, which is ten tens in the tens column.

This is expressed as zero in the tens column, and a one appears in the hundreds column.

ONE hundred is the same as TEN tens or ONE HUNDRED units.

The number 5000 could be expressed as four thousands and ten hundreds, as ten hundreds equals one thousand.

Five hundred is the same as fifty tens, (ten tens equals one hundred, so twenty tens equals two hundred ... so fifty tens equals five hundred).

EXERCISES:
How many
(d) hundreds in 2300 ?
(e) tens in 125 ?
(f) thousands in 13,857 ?

Understanding the structure of our number system will help in calculating subtractions involving 3 or more digits, and in long division.

ANSWERS TO THE EXERCISES:
(a) 429,008
(b) 5,088,056
(c) 1,766
(d) 23
(e) 12
(f) 13

Chapter 6

MORE ADVANCED SUBTRACTIONS

Having studied the structure of our number system and place value, I feel we are now ready to tackle subtractions involving 3 or more digits and zeros. The following examples show a more advanced subtraction solved by using three methods.

$$
\begin{array}{r}
2\,0\,0\,1 \\
-\quad 9\,9 \\
\hline
\end{array}
$$

DECOMPOSITION

STEP 1:

i. In the units column, nine from one I can't do, so I have to adjust a neighbouring column.

ii. The nearest column of any help is the thousands; the rest have only zeros.

$$
\begin{array}{r}
\cancel{2}\,{}^{1}0\,0\,1 \\
-\quad 9\,9 \\
\hline
\end{array}
$$

iii. Take one of the thousands, which leaves one behind, and change it to ten hundreds.

iv. Transfer these ten hundreds to the hundreds column. This has still not helped me with the calculation.

STEP 2:

i. Take one of these hundreds, leaving nine behind, and change it to ten tens.

$$
\begin{array}{r}
{}^{1}\;{}^{9} \\
\not{2}\,{}^{1}\not{0}\,{}^{1}0\;1 \\
-\quad 9\;9 \\
\hline
\end{array}
$$

ii. Transfer these ten tens into the tens column. This still has not helped me with the calculation.

STEP 3:

i. Take one of these tens, leaving nine behind, and change it to ten units.

$$
\begin{array}{r}
{}^{1}\;{}^{9}\;{}^{9} \\
\not{2}\,{}^{1}\not{0}\,{}^{1}\not{0}\,{}^{1}1 \\
-\quad 9\;9 \\
\hline
1\,9\,0\,2
\end{array}
$$

ii. Transfer these ten units to the units column.

iii. Ten units plus one unit gives eleven units, and I can now do the subtraction!

In the units column: $11 - 9 = 2$
In the tens column: $9 - 9 = 0$
In the hundreds column : $9 - 0 = 9$
In the thousands column: $1 - 0 = 1$

EQUAL ADDITION

STEP 1: IN THE UNITS COLUMN,

i. Nine from one I can't do.

$$2\ 0\ 0\ {}^1 1$$
$$-\ \ 9\ 9$$
$$\underline{\qquad {}^1 \qquad}$$
$$2$$

ii. I add ten to the top in the units column, giving eleven units, *and* ten to the bottom in the tens column (which shows as 1 under the tens column).

iii. Nine from eleven is two.

STEP 2: IN THE TENS COLUMN,

i. Nine tens plus one ten equals ten tens

$$2\ 0\ {}^1 0\ {}^1 1$$
$$-\ \ 9\ 9$$
$$\underline{\quad {}^1\ {}^1 \quad}$$
$$0\ 2$$

ii. Ten from zero I can't do, so add ten tens to the top, in the tens column, *and* ten tens to the bottom in the next column.

iii. Since ten tens are one hundred, the ten added to the bottom shows as 1 under the hundreds column.

iv. Ten from ten is zero.

STEP 3: IN THE HUNDREDS COLUMN,

i. One from zero I can't do

ii. Add ten hundreds to the top, in the hundreds column, *and* ten hundreds to the bottom in the next column.

$$2^10^10^11$$
$$-\ \ 99$$
$$\underline{1\ \ 1\ \ 1}$$
$$9\ 0\ 2$$

iii. Since ten hundreds are one thousand, the ten added to the bottom shows as 1 under the thousands column.

iv. One from ten is nine.

STEP 4: IN THE THOUSANDS COLUMN

i. One from two is one.

$$2^10^10^11$$
$$-\ \ 99$$
$$\underline{1\ \ 1\ \ 1}$$
$$1\ 9\ 0\ 2$$

Once again please remember that both methods are valid, but they are quite different. Try using both methods yourself.

SUBTRACTION BY ADDITION
(COMPLEMENTARY ADDITION)

The calculation 2001-99 is as follows,
   99 to 101 is 2
   101 to 1001 is 900
   1001 to 2001 is 1000
   2 + 900 + 1000 is 1902

Please note, there are a number of other suitable stages
that could have been used instead for this calculation.

Chapter 7

DIVISION: SHARE AND SHARE ALIKE?

After discovering I had been hoodwinked by subtraction, I found myself asking what I was actually doing when calculating a long division. I had been taught how to calculate a long division by following a set of rules. Some parents are puzzled by the way long division is now taught in some schools. Is it really that different?

Let's start with how many like myself were taught long division by using the following example.

$$632 \div 23 \qquad \text{or} \qquad 23 \overline{\smash{)}632}$$

STEP 1
We considered the first digit, 6: was it divisible by 23? We said that 23 into 6 does not go, so we left a blank above the 6.

$$23 \quad \overline{\smash{)}6\,3\,2}$$

STEP 2
We then considered the first two digits, 63: were they

divisible by 23? "Does 23 go into 63?" we asked. We decided, possibly after trial and improvement, that it goes 2 times. We wrote 2 directly above the 3 of the 63. We then calculated the multiplication 2x23=46, and found the remainder from 63 was 17.

```
      2
2 3 ⌐6 3 2
    4 6
    ───
    1 7
```

STEP 3
We then brought down the next number, and put it next to the remainder, making the number 172. Was this new number divisible by 23? "Does 23 go into 172?" we asked. Yes, (probably after more experiments in the margin) it goes 7 times. We then wrote 7 next to the 2, directly above the 2 of the 632, and worked out the multiplication 7 x 23 = 161. We found the remainder, in this case it is eleven.

```
      2 7
2 3 ⌐6 3 2
    4 6
    ───
    1 7 2
    1 6 1
    ─────
      1 1
```

Since there are no more numbers to consider, that completed the calculation. The answer is 27 remainder 11 (written as 27 r11).

Now division can be seen as a way of repeatedly subtracting. Let's look at the same division in this light. The 23 children at Gemma's party are to share a box of 632 sweets. How many does each get?

2 3 ⟌6 3 2	632 sweets to be shared
2 3	1 sweet to every child uses up 23 sweets
6 0 9	609 sweets left
2 3 0	10 sweets each speeds things up, uses 230
3 7 9	379 sweets left
2 3 0	10 sweets each again, uses further 230
1 4 9	149 sweets left
1 3 8	6 sweets to every child uses up 138
1 1	11 sweets remain.

27 sweets are given to each child

I have subtracted 23, 27 times, with remainder 11. In other words 632 ÷ 23 = 27 r11.

In this method, which has been taught in some of our schools, the complete number to be divided is involved for the whole calculation.

EXPLAINING LONG DIVISION

In the first method, we also subtracted batches of 23, but we systematically split up the number. Once we grasp what is in the number 632, and see it in terms of

100's, 10's and units, we can see the division in a different way:

2 individual sweets

+ 3 bags, each bag contains 10 sweets

+ 6 boxes, each box contains 10 bags (100 sweets)

600 + 30 + 2 = 632

OR

63 bags, each has 10 sweets

+ 2 individual sweets

630 + 2 = 632

OR

632 individual sweets

and the first method becomes clearer.

STEP 1

In considering the 6, we are actually considering 6 hundreds, and asking does 23 go into, "fit into", 6 hundreds. In our example of the bags of sweets, there are 6 boxes each containing 100. Can 23 go into these 6? Are there enough of these boxes for at least one each? NO.

$$2\,3\,\overline{)6\,3\,2}$$

STEP 2

i. We think of the number in smaller units. 6 hundreds is 60 tens. In considering the first two digits, 63, we are actually thinking of the number in tens. We are considering 63 tens, and asking does 23 go into, "fit into", 63 tens.

ii. In our example of the bags of sweets, we have opened the 6 boxes, taken out the bags of 10 and have now made 60 bags. There were already 3 bags of ten, so altogether there are 63 bags of ten.

iii. Can 23 go into, "fit into", these 63? YES, it goes in twice. Each child gets 2 of these bags, 46 are used and 17 remain. Looking at the calculation again, the answer to the question, "Does 23 go into 63?", is YES, it goes in twice. We subtract (2 x 23 = 46) 46 from the 63, and get a remainder of 17 tens. We wrote the 2 directly above the 3, by doing this we gave it a place value of 2 tens, as we were considering the number as in tens.

$$
\begin{array}{r}
2 \\
23\overline{)632} \\
46 \\
\hline
17
\end{array}
$$

STEP 3

i. Once again we think of the number in smaller units. We bring down the next number. What we are actually doing is adding the next number 2 to the remainder 17 tens or one hundred and seventy units, giving 172 units.

ii. In our example of the sweets, we have opened up the bags of ten. Since there were 17 of them, we now have 170 individual sweets, there are two sweets which were not in the bags of ten, so altogether we have 172 sweets.

Can 23 go into,"fit into", these 172? YES, it goes in 7 times.

iii. Each child gets 7 of these individual sweets, and 11 are left over.

```
        2 7
  2 3 | 6 3 2
      4 6
      ─────
      1 7 2
      1 6 1
      ─────
        1 1
```

Looking at the calculation again, the answer to the question, "Does 23 go into 172?", is YES, it goes in 7 times. We subtract (7 x 23 = 161) 161 from the 172, and got a remainder of 11. We wrote the 7 directly above the 2, by doing this we gave it the place value 7 units, as we were considering the number to be in units.

The final answer is 27 r11.

This method lends itself very easily to decimal division.

For further reading on the subject of division, see the references at the back of this book.

Part 3

HELPING YOUR CHILD

Chapter 8

BUILDING CONFIDENCE

"Maths needs to be a celebration of what is right," said the maths coordinator for a local junior school. I found this comment rather interesting.

Unfortunately, there is often a lot of concentration on what someone has got wrong, not what they have got right. Perhaps the reason for this is that in mathematics, right and wrong show up more starkly than in any other subject I can think of.

If a pupil keeps getting things wrong, their confidence and self-esteem can be brought down very low. This destroys their enthusiasm for the subject, and it becomes more difficult for them to learn. This can easily become a vicious circle.

HOW TO BE POSITIVE WHEN MISTAKES OCCUR

When your child gets something wrong, it is important for you and for them to see the mistakes as a springboard for something positive, an opportunity to increase their understanding. Do not just say, "You have got that wrong, this is how you do it." Instead:

i. Find out where they are; find out what they are thinking and where they have gone wrong. Ask them, "Tell me, how did you get that answer?" As they discuss their thinking with you, any areas of error, misconception, misunderstanding and so on, will become apparent.

ii. Show them where they went wrong and help them to correct the mistake. If all you had done was to say, "That's wrong, do this," then you would not have found out the root of the problem.

iii. Communicate that getting the question wrong has been very useful. After all, it has shown up an area that needed more attention.

COMMON STUMBLING BLOCKS

The following are some of the areas that often come up. This is by no means an exhaustive list!

i. *Misunderstanding an instruction. The child has half-learnt or not fully understood a procedure, and so keeps making an error in a simple operation.*
   One pupil I had was making the error shown in the example here:

$$\begin{array}{r} 6\,7\,5 \\ -\,4\,8\,9 \\ \hline 2\,1\,4 \\ \hline \end{array}$$

The answer is wrong. The answer should be 186. What has the pupil done here?

The pupil had misunderstood the instruction that to do a subtraction you take the smaller number away from the larger number. As you can see, they have followed that instruction for each column in isolation, even though the smaller number was in the top row. Research has shown that this is one of the seven most common mistakes[3] made when using a subtraction procedure.

Starting with place value, I revised with them how to work out a subtraction. Using ten pence and penny coins as a visual aid is a good idea.

In principle, once a misunderstanding has been pinpointed, the child then needs to be given the correct explanation.

ii. *The child may not fully understand the question and therefore choose the wrong operation. This can occur in problems expressed in words.*

I cannot offer a simple solution to this, as it depends on the exact question. However, I mention it to point out that the difficulty may not be in the maths at all!

iii. *The child may not understand what certain mathematical words or symbols mean.*

Some people find symbols such as ">" or "<" very off-putting, and do not know what they mean. Once again, start from where they are, and ask "Why did you do that? How did you work it out?" Or, "Do you know what all the symbols mean?" Encourage them that this is quite common, and they are not silly or stupid! Then explain what the terms or symbols or words mean. If possible, give everyday examples to describe what you are saying. These symbols are listed in the glossary at the back of this book.

iv. *They misread the question.*

Once again, asking the question, "How did you get that answer?" will show up whether there is a problem, or just that a slip has been made.

THE IMPORTANCE OF SELF-ESTEEM

Perhaps because maths is a subject in which it is very clear when you get something wrong, many people are made to feel unduly depressed about their performance and believe themselves to be "bad at maths". This belief tends to make further learning difficult, and it is important to avoid it. Getting things wrong can be a useful part of the learning process as long as your morale has not been broken. The importance of encouragement can hardly be overstated.

As I talk to people, I have become aware of how extraordinarily blessed I have been with the maths teachers I have had. I know others have not had such a good experience.

The one who had the most impact on my approach to maths was a teacher who only retired recently. She had taught in the same school for over 30 years.

One particularly memorable event was when she suddenly said, in the middle of a lesson, "Girls, I cannot see how to do this question at the moment. This is quite common in maths. If you can't see how to do it, leave it, and come back to it. Don't panic. Now, can anyone see how to do it?" There then followed a discussion, and there was indeed someone who could see how to do it, and they worked it out on the board.

My esteem of the teacher did not fall because she admitted to not being able to see at first what to do. On the contrary, being in a class with this sort of atmosphere, where one could admit to not knowing what to do, has obviously been very helpful to me.

I often tell my pupils about this incident to encourage them not to panic when faced with a question which they have no idea at first how to tackle, and also not to feel bad about it.

BUILDING SELF-ESTEEM

As we have already discussed, if there has been a lot of failure at maths, a pupil's self-esteem can be brought down and this is not helpful in learning the subject. For example, if they have a low opinion of their maths ability, they may think it is because of this that they are having difficulties, and not bother to ask the quite reasonable questions they have.

Let us be clear, maths is a challenging subject, and at times it is hard work. However, the difficulties which arise may not be due to a person's inability.

Here are some tips on how to build up self-esteem in maths.

i. *Encourage the pupil that if they have seemingly simple queries, these are important; find an opportunity to clarify them.*

As a tutor, I am usually dealing with pupils on a one-to-one basis. In this confidential situation, I tell my students that no question is too simple to ask. I am not going to shout at them or bite their head off!

ii. *They may need another approach.*

If I have explained something and it does not make sense, I reassure the pupil that it may not be their fault. I could have explained it in a way that is not suitable for them. I ask them to be honest and say if they do not understand, as I will just find another way of explaining things. There is often more than one way of tackling a problem. An explanation that suits one person need not necessarily suit another.

If I were to ask how to get to London from my home in Dorset, I am sure many routes could be found. The shortest, the most scenic, the safest, the quickest, the longest ... to name a few. Is there only one right way? Of course not! Similarly, there may be many ways of tackling a maths problem. We need to find the way that suits the child.

Indeed, as we have seen in our discussion about the National Curriculum, children are to be encouraged to see that there is a variety of ways of tackling a problem.

iii. *Others have probably had the same problem too.*

I believe that pupils find it very reassuring to know that others have had the same problem. If there is one thing I would like to say to all those who did not understand something and did not have the courage to ask, it is this: "There were probably lots of others in the same boat – if only you knew!"

My advice is that if a problem arises, ask the teacher about it at a suitable point. It does not have to be in front of everyone else. Perhaps at the end of the lesson, or when you can catch them on their own.

iv. *Fill in the missing "building blocks".*

Realising that they have missed a "building block", and therefore that something can be done is a terrific boost for self-esteem. I have already discussed in the introduction reasons for this occurring, such as missing school.

Backtrack to the point they did understand and start from there. It may mean asking the teacher for work to do with the child to make up lost ground, or having extra lessons for a short period with a maths specialist to catch up. Discuss the matter with their teacher who may be able to recommend a suitable person.

HOW TO FIND THE MISSING "BUILDING BLOCKS"

One simple way of doing this is to ask them, "If you had a choice of maths questions, which ones would you leave out?"

Asking why these areas were chosen often leads on to discussion of where the difficulties are. These areas can then be addressed.

CONFIDENCE

I cannot stress too much the importance of praising what is right. Let us say a pupil suggests a way of approaching a problem. If only part of what they say is correct, I tend to pick that up and comment and give praise for that first. I generally give praise that a strategy is correct *first* before commenting on other issues. Obviously, if it is totally wrong, you need to be honest and say so, but be gentle about it.

I feel the key is to celebrate what is right, and start from there.

Chapter 9

Maths As Part Of Everyday Life

One comment I keep hearing from people is that they could never see the point of maths lessons at school.

It would seem they could not make a connection between the work they did at school, and everyday life It all seemed very remote.

In fact, the mere mention of the fact that I am a maths specialist normally provokes an awe in others, and a feeling that I must be some sort of alien. It usually brings a hush to the conversation, and comments such as, "I was never any good at maths at school."

The fact is many of us are making mathematical decisions as part of our daily life without even realising it!

So, you can be doing maths with your child without sitting them down and doing reams and reams of abstract sums.

Making maths part of everyday life is very helpful. Often, these days, real life situations are used in the maths questions your child is asked to do.

I understand that teachers often find children are not getting practice at handling money. Shopping habits these days mean that sweets and crisps are bought at a supermarket, as part of the big family shopping. Usually these are paid for by cheque or credit card, and children are not getting practice at handling money. This is one important area in which you can help your child. The following are just some of the fun activities you can do with your child, as you go about your daily life.

IN THE CAR

* Collect car numbers. Who collected the most/fewest? Put your collection in order. Which is the highest/lowest? What is the difference between them?

* Read the milometer at the start and end of the journey. How many miles were covered?

* Which colour car is the most popular? Stand inside your gate for 10 minutes and record the colour of each car that passes. Repeat every day for a week. What did you find out?

IN THE SHOPS

* Hunt for the most expensive item/cheapest item in the shop. Find the difference.

* Use the supermarket till receipt. Find the average cost of the items. Use the receipt to find what can be

bought for £5.

*   Write the cost of each item on a separate piece of paper, turn them over and muddle the pieces up. Choose three items, add up the cost and say what change would be given from £5/£10.

*   If multi-packs are bought, what is the cost of one packet? How much do you save buying multi-packs?

*   If you only had 2p and 5p coins, how would you pay for different priced items exactly? (I will add an aside here: Are there any you cannot pay for?)

*   Look at "sell-by" dates on the shopping and put them in order. What items have the shortest shelf-life?

*   Make a collection of examples of price reductions (or increases) by a given percentage. How much is saved?

PACKAGING

*   Convert metric to imperial to get a feel for the equivalents.

*   Collect some interesting packages. Draw what you think the net (the shape opened out) will look like, then open up the package and see if you were right.

*   Choose one interesting package and construct one,

using a net, where all the lengths are halved (or scale of 1:2). Construct the shapes using geometric tools such as pairs of compasses, rulers, etc.

SPECIAL OCCASIONS

* You are having a birthday party. Plan the food you will have for your friends. What will it cost for each item/altogether? What will the prizes, party bags and balloons, etc. cost?

* Planning holidays. Distances, prices, average temperatures, etc.

* Changing currency for holidays. Collect prices of small items bought abroad and find out the cost in sterling – if prices are in sterling, what might they cost in French francs, guilders, etc?

EXPLORING TIME

* How long have you been alive in years, in months, in weeks, in days, etc?

* You have a 180 minute video. As you will be on holiday with no television for a week, you want to record your favourite programmes. Which ones will you record and how much of the 180 minutes will be used?

SCALE

* Measure your bedroom and draw it to one tenth scale on 1 cm squared paper. Measure and draw your furniture to the same scale and put it in the correct places. What is the area of the bedroom? What area is covered by furniture?

COOKING

* There is a lot of scope for measuring fractions of quantities. For example, half the Victoria sponge mixture is put in one tin, the other half in the other tin.

* Adapt a recipe for more/less people, and cook it.

PLAYING BOARD GAMES AND CARD GAMES

* Playing various card games, such as Pontoon (practises adding up to 21 among other things), and Patience (practises ordering numbers).

* Board games such as Snakes and Ladders, Backgammon, Monopoly ...

MISCELLANEOUS PUZZLES

* Explore the following query, "The answer is 10, what was the question?"

* Together, try playing Spiders. An example of one game is shown below:

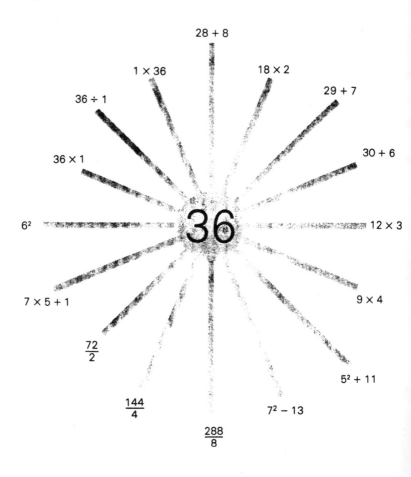

Spiders:

Someone suggests a starting number and everyone supplies a fact about it which is entered in a radial form.

The idea is that patterns should be noted and used to generate more and more mathematical facts.

This activity can also be made competitive by asking individuals to enter as many facts as possible in a limited time.

I am very grateful to Diana Cobden, a Maths Advisor for Dorset, for allowing me to use extracts from her excellent booklet, "Helping Children With Maths At Home", for the areas of: In the car, In the shops, Packaging, Special Occasions, Exploring Time and Scale. Also to The Mathematical Association for use of "Spiders", from their publication, "Sharing Mathematics With Parents".

Chapter 10

MULTIPLICATION

WHAT IS MULTIPLICATION?

How would you answer that question?

It would appear to me, from conversations I have had, that people have successfully learnt their multiplication "times tables", but not understood what they mean.

During Key Stage 1, there is provision in the programme of study for the following:

"Pupils should be taught to understand the operations of multiplication, and division ..." (National Curriculum p.4)

What is multiplication? For what we are considering here, it is basically repeated addition.

4 x 3 = 12

means that if you add 3 together 4 times you get 12.

3 + 3 + 3 + 3 = 12

HOW IT IS TAUGHT

This would probably be shown to the children very

practically, for example, they may see a diagram of a bird's nest with 3 eggs in it. How many eggs would there be if there were 4 such nests?

Answer: 3 + 3 + 3 + 3 = 12

Or, we say, 4 times 3 is 12, and write 4 x 3 = 12

I know of one parent who could not understand why her son was spending so much time adding up groups of three. Hopefully, this will help to clarify what pupils are doing!

WHY DO THEY NEED TO UNDERSTAND WHAT MULTIPLICATION IS?

It is important to understand what multiplication is, so that you will be able to apply it when faced with an appropriate problem. It also means that if you cannot remember your "multiplication times tables", you can work out what you need.

DO CHILDREN STILL LEARN "TABLES"?

Yes, they do. During Key Stage 2, there is provision in the programme of study for the following:

"Pupils should be taught to know the multiplication facts to 10x10; to develop a range of mental methods for finding quickly from known facts those that they cannot recall ..."
(National Curriculum, Number, p.7)

Notice that they should also have strategies of how

to work out those they cannot recall. For example, they may know $7 \times 8 = 56$, but cannot remember what 8×8 is. Since multiplication is repeated addition, adding 8 to 56 will give the required answer of 64.

It is worth noting that it does not matter which way around you do the multiplication, you will arrive at the same answer.

$3 \times 4 = 12$

$4 \times 3 = 12$

This is very encouraging to know when learning "tables", as this almost halves the number of multiplications you need to learn!

Chapter 11

PART OF THE PICTURE: FRACTIONS, DECIMALS, PERCENTAGES

In this section, I am going to discuss what can be loosely described as parts of a whole.

Generally, the approach to teaching this area is through lots of practical work, once again involving everyday situations. Parents can help enormously.

FRACTIONS

The important thing is for children to understand the concept of a fraction, and to be able to recognise fractions. They start with simple ones, such as halves and quarters. Parents can help by doing activities such as cooking with their children.

In baking a Victoria sponge, half the mixture goes in one tin; the other half goes in another. They are seeing at first hand what a half means.

Adapting recipes is a very useful way for parents to help in this important area. For example, say the recipe is for 8, how will you adapt it for 4? Then have a go at cooking it together.

DECIMALS

Shopping is a very good way of introducing decimals! One approach used in teaching this area is to look at the cost of things. Children see the cost as being whole pounds, and bits of a pound, and gradually build up from this.

Measuring using metric units such as metres is another way to introduce this important area.

PERCENTAGES

Let us remember that percentages can be described as fractions with a denominator ("the number at the bottom") of 100.

So, 30% is the same as $^{30}/_{100}$, which is also $^{3}/_{10.}$

Once again, practical ways of getting across the idea of percentages would probably be used. This needs to be related to everyday life. Since percentages are often quoted in the media, there are ample opportunities for discussion.

One way that parents could help is in the basic foundations of being able to recognise parts of a whole, and use simple percentages to describe them. For example, serve up 25% of a pizza (it is the same as a quarter of the pizza).

Chapter 12

BALANCING TRICKS:
A LOOK AT SIMPLE ALGEBRA

Before we look at some basic algebra, we need to revise a few facts.

If I start with 3 apples, and add 2 apples, I get 5 apples. To get back to where I started, I would have to take away the 2 apples.

Similarly, if I start with 10 apples and take away 3 apples, I would have 7 apples. To get back to the number of apples I started with, I would have to add 3 apples.

To summarise, if I *subtract* a number, then to get back to where I started, I would have to *add* the same number.

Similarly, if I *add* a number, then I would have to *subtract* the same number to get to the original number.

Let us say I think of a number, then double it (multiply it by 2). To get back to where I started, I would have to divide the answer by 2. For example,

$$2 \times 10 = 20$$
$$20 \div 2 = 10$$

Similarly, if I divide a number by 3, to get back to the number I started with, I would multiply the answer by 3.

36 ÷ 3 = 12
12 x 3 = 36

Having established these connections between addition and subtraction, and between multiplication and division, let us turn our minds to the following problem.

FORMING EQUATIONS

I think of a number, then double it, then add 3. My answer is 9, what was the original number?

The problem could be written down like this, where "a" is standing in for the unknown number.

i. a is the number I start with. I double it. I can do this by multiplying 2 x a which gives $2a$

ii. I then add 3, so I now have $2a + 3$

iii. this equals 9, which I write as

$$2a + 3 = 9$$

I have written it down in what is known as an equation.

BALANCING EQUATIONS

Equations are like weighing scales. If you tamper with one side, you have to give the other side the same treatment if you wish them to remain in balance.

Look at the pictures over the page. In the first picture, the scales are in balance. In the second, they have gone out of balance because one side has been tampered with.

If I remove anything from one side, I will have to remove the same amount from the other side to keep the balance.

SOLVING EQUATIONS

To find out the number a I originally thought of, think of the equation like the scales in the diagram, with $2a + 3$ in one pan, and 9 in the other pan.

At present, they are balanced. By suitably adjusting both pans, I want eventually to end up with only a in one pan, and a number in the other pan, with the scales being balanced. Then I will have solved the problem, as I have a value for a.

The last thing I did was to add 3, so to get to the stage before that, I subtract 3.

I subtract 3 from the left hand side, and will have to do the same to the right hand side to keep the scales in balance:

$$2a + 3 = 9$$

$2a + 3 - 3 = 9 - 3$
$+ 3 - 3 = 0$, so:
$2a = 9 - 3$
$2a = 6$

We are now at the stage where we have thought of the number and multiplied it by 2.

To get back to the original number, divide BOTH sides by 2, as we want to keep things balanced:

$^{2a}/_2 = {}^6/_2$
$2a \div 2 = a$ and $6 \div 2 = 3$, so
$a = 3$

3 is the number I originally thought of.

A HANDY RULE OF THUMB, BUT ...

What I have shown is what is actually going on, and is a method used these days to teach algebra.

Parents may not recognise what I have just done. They may recollect solving equations using a number of rules such as, "Change the side, change the sign."

That rule is in fact a mechanism which achieves the same result: it is not the real process, as can be shown in our example:

$$2a + 3 = 9$$
$$2a + 3 - 3 = 9 - 3$$
$$2a = 9 - 3$$

The +3 seems to have "disappeared" from the left and "reappeared" on the right as -3. It appears to have "changed side" and "changed sign". The rule portrays the operation as a sort of conjuring trick: a close look at the middle line will show that the 3 on the right hand side is not the same 3 as the one that was on the left hand side.

"Change the side, change the sign," is a very handy rule of thumb, but it is obscuring what is really going on and may give the impression that maths is a series of unreasonable tricks (see my comment in Chapter One!).

I grant that the full explanation which I set out above may look laborious. I have written out all the steps, but after a while some of them will be dropped.

It is important to grasp the principles of balancing equations, rather than just learning a rule.

$3b - 4 = 14$

Here is another example:

Kelly bought 3 multi-packs of crisps. She packed 4 individual bags into lunchboxes, and now has 14 individual bags left. How many individual bags make up a multi-pack?

Let b stand for the number of individual bags in a multi-pack.

Since Kelly bought 3 multi-packs, there are:

$b + b + b = 3b$ number of bags

She used 4 in lunchboxes, and was left with 14:

$3b - 4 = 14$

Let us solve the equation to find b,

$3b - 4 + 4 = 14 + 4$

$3b = 18$

$^{3b}/_3 = {}^{18}/_3$

$b = {}^{18}/_3 = 6$

There are 6 bags in one multi-pack.

Try these exercises:

(a) Sara bought 7 chews and a toffee bar costing 10p. The total bill was 31p. How much did each chew cost?

(Hint: let "a" stand for the cost of each chew. Then: $7a + 10 = 31$, find a.)

(b) Luke had £8 in his pocket. He bought 3 rollerball pens. He now has £2 left. How much were the rollerball pens?

(Hint: if x is the cost of each pen, then $8 - 3x = 2$, find x.)

Answers:

(a) $7a + 10 = 31$
$7a + 10 - 10 = 31\text{-}10$
$7a = 21$
$a = {}^{21}/_7$
$a = 3$

(b) $8 - 3x = 2$
$8 - 3x + 3x = 2 + 3x$
$8 = 2 + 3x$
$8 - 2 = 2 - 2 + 3x$
$6 = 3x$
${}^6/_3 = x$
$2 = x$

which is the same as:
$x = 2$

That last step should be obvious, because the two sides are equal and are therefore interchangeable. However, in case that last step worries you, I could say that I have subtracted x from both sides, subtracted 2 from both sides, and multiplied both sides by -1.

Chapter 13

USE OF CALCULATORS: A CALCULATED RISK?

FALLING NUMERACY STANDARDS?

The use of calculators is probably one of the most controversial areas for parents ... among other people!

The fear is that in using calculators, numeracy standards are falling.

IMPORTANCE OF ESTIMATION

It needs to be remembered that in connection with the use of calculators, children are taught to estimate their answer. This is so that they can see whether the answer they get from the calculation is reasonable.

"In solving problems with or without a calculator, pupils check the reasonableness of their results by reference to their knowledge of the context or to the size of the numbers." (National Curriculum, Number and Algebra, Level 4, p.25)

In calculating an estimation, they actually have to use some or all of the operations of " + ", " - ", " x " and " ÷ ".

NO EASY ANSWERS!

The person operating the calculator also has to work out exactly what needs to be done. I finish this book with the following crossword, reproduced by permission of the Mathematical Association from their publication, "Sharing Mathematics With Parents".

It demonstrates that no machine can produce the required answers until the operator has worked out what to do!

Calculator crossword

Some numbers on the calculator spell words, if you turn the calculator round to read them. The answers to this crossword are all words but the clues over the page give you the numbers to make them.

Clues across

1. The creature in 6 across may be sore but at least they are not 5 million more than 537 637.

4. Just $^1/_2$

6. 400 millipedes have lost 20 096 legs. What must they do on those they have left?

8. $11 + (6^2 \times 157)$ of these should not be put in one basket

9. $7 + 8^2$ Watch out, it is French.

10. $75^2 + 45^2 + 8^2$ is a lump of ground.

11. Look at all those people:
  5 regiments each with
  27 companies of
  269 soldiers. What's happening?

12. 37 hundredths is a lion of a number.

Clues down

2. 20% of 1 883 080 is no laughing matter.

3. David ate 5 sweets and gave 40 to each of his 20 friends. Now he has none left, what does he do?

4. Once upon a time Miss Muffett bought 221 shares for £1 each. Now they are each worth £36. What does the profit tell her to do?

5. By mistake the school ordered 7 boxes each containing 7 packets of 113 sheets of blotting paper. Look at what arrived and say what was wanted.

7. Jack and who climbed 10 across? Add 4 to that answer to find out.

10. Who's $2^5 + 2$? The cat's grandfather?

Now make up some of your own clues.

REFERENCES

Chapter 2
1. "Mathematics 5-11 A Handbook of Suggestions" HMI Series: Matters for Discussion,HMSO 1979, page 1. (Italics mine.) Crown copyright is reproduced with the permission of the Controller of HMSO.
2. Ibid. page 7. (Italics mine.)

Chapter 4
Ibid. pages 30-1.

Chapter 7 (Division)
Mathematics to Level 10: A Full GCSE Course, L.Bostock, S.Chandler, A.Shepherd and E.Smith, Stanley Thornes, Cheltenham 1994, page 5.
HBJ Mathematics Y5, page 93; *HBJ Mathematics Teacher's Resource Book*, page 207, Harcourt Brace Jovanovich Limited 1992.
"Mathematics 5-11 A Handbook of Suggestions" HMI Series: Matters for Discussion, HMSO 1979, pages 32-3.

Chapter 8
3. Resnick,L.B. (1982) "Syntax and Semantics in Learning to Subtract", in Carpenter, T.P. (Ed) *Addition and Subtraction: A Cognitive Perspective*, New Jersey, Lawrence Erlbaum; cited in Dickson, L., Brown, M. and Gibson,O. (1984) *Children Learning Mathematics: A Teacher's Guide to Recent Research*, London, Cassell, page 262.

FURTHER READING

The Psychology of Learning Mathematics, R.R.Skemp, reprinted in Penguin Books 1993.

"Mathematics 5-11 A Handbook of Suggestions", HMI Series:Matters for Discussion, HMSO 1979.

Sharing Maths Cultures: IMPACT: (Inventing Maths for Parents and Children and Teachers), Ruth Merttens and Jeff Vass, The Falmer Press 1990.

Sharing Mathematics with Parents, The Mathematical Association, Stanley Thornes 1989.

"Mathematics in the National Curriculum", HMSO 1995.

GLOSSARY OF TERMS

Algorithm
A procedure or a set of rules for working out a calculation.

Counting Numbers
See Numbers.

Denominator
See Fraction Even.

Difference
The answer to a subtraction.

Educationalist
An expert in educational methods (usually found in teacher training colleges rather than schools).

Even Number
See Numbers.

Factor
This is a number which divides exactly into a given number, with no remainder. For example, 4 is a factor of 12 as 4 divides exactly into 12 with no remainder.

Fraction
The word means part. As an example, if we claim that we can do a task in a fraction of the time in which someone else can do it, we are saying that we can do it in part of the time it takes them.

The bottom number of a fraction is called the *denominator* and tells us how many *equal* parts the whole has been divided into.

The top number of the fraction is called the *numerator* and tells us how many of the equal parts we are considering.

For example, $1/2$ of a bar of chocolate means we have split the bar into 2 equal parts, and 1 of these parts is being considered.

Integer
See Numbers.

Multiple
A multiple of a number is the number itself multiplied by any integer. For example, some multiples of 5 are 5, 10, 25, 60; some multiples of 7 are 7, 21, 35, 84.

Natural Numbers
See Numbers.

Numbers
Integers: These are all the positive and negative whole numbers and zero, i.e. ... -2, -1, 0, 1, 2, ... (zero is neither positive nor negative).

Natural Numbers: These are the positive integers, also known as the *Counting Numbers*, i.e. 1, 2, 3 ...

Even Numbers: These are the integers that are exactly divisible by 2, i.e. ... -6, -4, -2, 2, 4, 6, 8, 10 ... Every even number ends with 0, 2, 4, 6, or 8.

Odd Numbers: These are the integers that are not exactly divisible by 2., i.e. ... -5, -3, -1, 1, 3, 5, 7, 9, 11 ... Every odd number ends with 1, 3, 5, 7 or 9.

Prime Number: This is a positive integer which has precisely two distinct factors, the number itself and 1. For example, 2, 3, 5, 7, 11, 13, 17, ... Note, 1 is not a prime number.

Square Number: This is a positive integer which is the result of multiplying together two equal factors. For example, 3 x 3 = 9, 9 is a square number. We usually write this as, 3^2 = 9 Other examples of square numbers are 1, 4, 16, 25, 36, 49, ...

Numerator
See Fraction.

Product
The answer to a multiplication. For example, the product of 12 and 10 is 120.

Quotient
The answer to a division.

Square Root
When we write a number as the product of two equal factors, then each factor is called a square root of the number e.g. 2.25 = 1.5 x 1.5. 1.5 is the square root of 2.25.

Sum
The answer to an addition.

Symbols

=
is equal to

≈
is approximately equal to

\>
is greater than. For example, $4 > 2$, which says, "4 is greater than 2". Notice that the larger number is next to the wide side of the symbol, and the smaller number is next to the pointed side of the symbol.

\<
is less than. For example, $21 < 32$, which says,"21 is less than 32". Notice that the smaller number is next to the pointed side of the symbol, and the larger number is next to the wide side of the symbol.

≥
is greater than or equal to

≤
is less than or equal to

$\sqrt{}$
the square root symbol

OTHER BOOKS FOR PARENTS BY PICCADILLY PRESS

SPELLING FOR PARENTS
by Jo Phenix and Doreen Scott-Dunne

English spelling isn't as difficult or illogical as it seems once you understand it. Entertaining and easy to read, this practical guide for parents wanting to help their children to spell includes:

• an explanation of children's spelling development
• how to recognise children's strengths and weaknesses
• discussing children's progress effectively with teachers
• fascinating spelling trivia (did you know that William Caxton's "u" didn't work very well, so he changed it to "o" in words like done and wonder?)

"...offers refreshingly easy strategies for parents to use with children encountering difficulties with spelling ... An optimistic book which would also be useful to adults with spelling problems" –
The Independent

GRAMMAR FOR PARENTS
by Jerry George with Clare Stuart

This is essential for any parent who wants to help their child with grammar. It includes: clear definitions of the terms we use to talk about grammar; explanations and examples of the major rules; suggestions for using grammar creatively to improve writing; and a list of the main grammar pitfalls.

READING FOR PARENTS
by Irene Yates

It's never too early or too late to help your child with reading! Find out:
- How children learn to read and how reading ability is affected by different skills and practice.
- Ways of making reading fun for your child through activities and games.
- The benefits and faults of reading schemes.
- How to recognise problems, help your child with specific difficulties, and enlist the support of your child's teachers.

ARE YOU EXPECTING TOO MUCH FROM YOUR CHILD
by Dr Fiona Subotsky

Do you spend a great deal of time worrying about your child? Have you ever considered that your aims may be beyond the reach or perhaps beyond the interest of your child? Do you notice family traits in your child?

Every child deserves to be accepted for who they are not what their parents want them to be. In this book, Fiona Subotsky draws parents' attention to their own behaviour and expectations, which might have a negative effect on their child's development.

Well Done
by Ken Adams

Your child can't be brilliant at everything! Most children have an area of weakness – verbal, mathematical or conceptual. Identify your child's weaknesses and help your child strengthen skills in these areas – without him or her even knowing.

Find out: how children learn, how they fails, specific difficulties arising in children up to the age of eleven and what you can do to help them.